TAKE THIS LIFE

Anne Tannam

6tHouse

First published in 2011 by
6tHouse
an imprint of Wordsonthestreet
Six San Antonio Park,
Salthill,
Galway, Ireland.
web: www.wordsonthestreet.com
email: publisher@wordsonthestreet.com

The moral right of the author has been asserted.
A catalogue record for this book is available from the British Library.

ISBN   978-1-907017-06-3

Cover design, layout and typesetting: Wordsonthestreet
Cover image: Laura Butler
Printed and bound in the UK

TAKE THIS LIFE

ABOUT THE AUTHOR

It may have taken Anne Tannam forty four years to write her first poetry collection *Take This Life* but she's been gathering material for it since the day she was born. And she's not fussy about where she finds her inspiration. It could be in the lyric of a song, or a well written sentence, a snatch of childish conversation, or the syntax of a poem.

Language has always fascinated Anne and whatever work she is doing, the importance of how we tell stories and connect with each other remains a constant. In her various roles as teacher, lifecoach and parent, language sits centre stage and endeavouring to employ it honestly and effectively is all in a day's work.

"Poetry can tell us what human beings are. It can tell us why we stumble and fall and how, miraculously we can stand up" Maya Angelou.

When Anne began to write herself, poetry seemed a natural choice as no other form of writing communicates so succinctly the unique but shared experience of being human.

Anne has performed her poetry at open mic nights across Dublin. She has read at the Glór Sessions, Seven Towers Last Wednesday Series, Wurm in Apfel, The Tongue Box and The Winding Stair. Anne has performed and discussed her work with Niamh Bagnell on Liffey Sounds.

For more information on Anne, please visit her website at annetannam.com

For Betty and Des who made everything possible

ACKNOWLEDGEMENTS

Thank you to everyone who nudged this book along. To Neil who gave me space and time and to Claire, Aislinn, Sian and Darragh for keeping my feet firmly on the ground.

A very special thanks to Jennifer who coaxed and cajoled the book into existence, to Frank who steadied me and to Patricia who uttered the magic words "When are you going to write books"?

Thanks to all the people who read the various drafts of the book and gave their excellent feedback, Bob, Celia, Eoin, Frank, Gerard, Geraldine, Jennifer, Liz, Maggie, Niamh, Nicki, Patricia and Tricia.

Thanks to Rebecca O'Connor at The Writer's Consultancy for her kind comments and suggestions.

Thank you to Laura Butler, an artist of integrity and generosity.

And finally, last but not least, thank you to 6tHouse for taking a chance.

The Story So Far

In September 2008, I ran out of reasons why I could not write (too busy, not good enough, no decent subject matter etc) and committed to turning up every day at the computer for at least an hour to see what might happen. So I turned up and slowly but steadily the poems began to flow and my written voice grew confident. A very good friend of mine offered to critique the work for me and her support and editorial advice was and continues to be, a godsend.

A year later the idea for the book came to me. Running through many of my poems was the theme of 'Life as Invitation' and so 'Take This Life' was born. I began to put together a first draft, using a mixture of poetry and prose. I asked six people to read it and give me feedback. The information I got back suggested that the poems themselves could stand alone, so for the next four months I worked on the second draft When I finished it in April, I sent it out to eighteen people for feedback.

I then sent the third draft to a professional editor and fellow poet. Her response was overwhelmingly positive. She suggested some minor changes which were in keeping with the tone and style of the book and I worked over the summer with her suggestions.

The next obvious step was to take the plunge and submit the book to a handful of publishing companies. In October I received an email which contained the lovely, lovely words "We would be pleased to publish this collection of poems". After a two year journey, my poems would finally be in print, safe and sound within the covers of this book. And now you hold it in your hands and the story so far continues onto the next chapter.

CONTENTS

No Linguistic Gymnastics Please   10
Take This Life   11
Circumnavigation   12
A Start   13
Paradise Lost and Found   14
All That is Required   15
A New Religion   16
Compare Yourself to No One   18
She is the One who Knows   19
Lucy   20
Transmutation   22
Transported   24
All the Good Words   25
Diminished   26
Memories   28
Can I Tell You About My Loves?   29
Between Us   30
The World Reduced to Sound   33
Post Excavation Analysis (and a little guesswork)   34
By the Time I Got There   36
The Medicine Bag   38
The Great Escape Part 1   40
Let it Breathe   42
She's Been Here Before   43
Journey   44
The Great Escape Part 2   46
Hugs   47
All Grown Up   48
A Hair's Breath   50

Like the Sun 51
Some Mornings I Wake 52
Waiting 54
The Great Escape Part 3 55
A Lopsided Conversation 56
Tuning In 57
The Art of Listening 60
The Start of the Affair 62
Her Absence 63
I Stand Outside 64
Doing Her Thing 65
Consolation 66
Reclaimed 68
Christmas Eve 70
The Woman in the Mirror 72
Curriculum Vitae 74
In an Ocean of Ignorance 75

No Linguistic Gymnastics Please

I just want the words to cushion me when I fall,
to sit with me a while until I catch my breath,
to hold my hand so I know I am not alone.

TAKE THIS LIFE

Take this life,
these circumstances,
the familiar ache,
the play of light that catches your eye,
a sleeping child,
a sudden loss,
the gift of tears,
the urge to dance when the house is quiet.
Take this life
and place it at the foot of the altar.
It is enough for now.

CIRCUMNAVIGATION

There are times when I'm in the thick of it,
using my three pairs of hands
to sauté onions,
stir fry vegetables
and scribble a list
of tedious ingredients
for tomorrow's dinner
and we're out of toothpaste,
I forget for a while the
earth has not been flat
for hundreds of years.
I forget we have already danced on the moon,
run rings around Saturn
and landed on Mars.

Remembering is like a small wooden boat
with a white canvas sail
that calls to the oceans
to carry us over the crest of each wave,
to carry us over the curve of our world,
until we see the familiar shoreline
with the eyes of a traveller who's been longing for home.

Behind the drone of the extractor fan,
far beyond the walls of my landlocked house,
I think I hear the sea.

A START

After twenty years or more
of writing snatches and snippets
on pieces of tissue
with invisible ink,
I said goodbye to 'one day'.

And 'one day' became 'that day'
when a ball of words untangled,
unravelling a tight knot.
With the loose yarn,
I decided to take up knitting.

'That day' became 'the day'
when the words burst their bank,
seeped onto a page
and left a pattern on it.
I saw a picture in the watermark.

And 'the day' became 'each day'
a jumble of images tumbled
about in my head
like playful puppies,
I trained them to sit still for a moment.

And 'a moment' becomes 'these moments'
when an image joins a feeling
and the words
reflect their union.
I dance like a mad thing at the wedding.

PARADISE LOST AND FOUND

The first boy I loved quoted poetry.
Walking side by side into town by Gardiner Street,
he ensnared me with softly spoken lines.
"Nobody, not even the rain, has such small hands".
So carried away was he by the sheer beauty of the poem,
he failed to mention his not quite ex girlfriend.
Maybe he just forgot her in the heat of the moment?
Anyway, my eighteen year old heart swooned
at the promise that such language holds.
A whole other universe opened up to me and I was
smitten.
I still am.
Though not of course by the thoughtless youth
who specialised in overlapping relationships.
(I wish him well, wherever he is)
It was just that when the pain of first love lost receded,
the language renewed its faithful promise to me
and the sensual sound of words that lingered on my lips
became my lover.
And still to this day we rise together
and still to this day walk hand in hand.

ALL THAT IS REQUIRED

All that is required
is to come to it,
stay with it,
go with it.

A NEW RELIGION

For years and years I prayed to a false god.
"Oh Mother of Perpetual Busyness,
bless your lowly servant and make her worthy".
Prostrate and hassled I lay at her altar,
bearing sacrifices and burnt offerings in the shape of my
life.

I wanted to please her, impress her, appease her
but nothing I did was ever enough.
Daily I worshipped the Deity of Duty
and chanted the mantra that kept me enthralled,
"Today I have to, must do, should do, serve you".
And I did.
Leaving my body a few steps behind,
my mind ran ahead, dashing this way and that,
creating lists that were endless and jobs that were pointless
but kept me from questioning
the tenets of my faith.

Until one day I heard of a new kind of religion
that practised the doctrine of 'That's Good Enough',
where my body and mind could walk at their own pace
and together they'd know which direction to take.
Now I pledge an oath of allegiance to the god of 'Take
your Time',
and I offer her nothing but the rhythm of my days
and the work that flows through each hour.

Thankfully my new god, my true god, 'It's up to you' god,
is easy to please and she gives of her blessings freely
and in my own time and at my own pace
I intend to please her daily
and accept the gift of her grace.

COMPARE YOURSELF TO NO ONE

Compare yourself to no one.
Nobody.
Not even another version of yourself.
There is no one in the world like you.
Allow yourself to relax,
to sit comfortably and easily
within the folds of who you are.
Settle into yourself and the light
will reflect from you,
like sunshine on the water's surface,
dancing, shimmering, rejoicing.
Ah, now I see you.

SHE IS THE ONE WHO KNOWS

There is a girl who lives inside me.
She is the one who knows how to fly.
With fearless abandon she swoops and soars
as I carefully keep to the middle of the road.

When I stand rooted to the motionless shore,
she skims across the endless seas
tumbling expertly with the waves.
Her rolling joy is a breathless cascade.

But in dreams we dance and play together
and I match her limb for laughing limb,
as we cartwheel across the carefree sky,
shifting and shaking the happy heavens.

LUCY

i
When I was just ten
and tightly furled,
Lucy came to play.
She took my hand
as the needle dropped
and whisked me far away.

ii
When I was just ten
and scared to fly,
Lucy called around.
She brought me wings
and a marmalade sky.
My feet never touched the ground.

iii
When I was just ten
and sang out of tune,
Lucy played a song
with Billy Shears
and the Lonely Hearts band.
She taught me to sing along.

iv
When I was just ten
and safe at home
Lucy ran away.
I was torn between
going or staying
and wrestled with it all day.

v
When I was just ten
with kaleidoscope eyes,
Lucy said goodbye,
but even now,
some thirty years on
I see diamonds in the sky.

TRANSMUTATION

On a midweek mitch from it's all too much,
I moseyed down to Collin's Barracks.
There was a temporary exhibition running called
'Modern Masterpieces from the Worshipful Company of
Goldsmiths'.
How could I resist?

Leaving outside the late morning sunshine I passed
through several doors into a hallowed space.
The walls were dark and black partitions, cleverly placed,
obscured the view and shielded the treasures from prying
eyes.
I padded across the silent carpet and rounded the corner
to sneak a peek into the cave. I wasn't disappointed.

With my eyes I heard the song of creation, sung in silver,
celebrating the marriage of metal and mastery.
With my ears I heard the light pour forth from each form
fashioned and it echoed in every corner of my mind.
I moved slowly from right to left, worshipping at each
small altar.
Unsure of how to pray, I stood in silence,
but found the words inscribed on tiny hymn sheets.
"Creased and hammered in thin gauge silver"
"Forged silver with Zirconin and ebony filial set with
amethysts"
"Horizontal fluting, hammered – on-air".

Within each piece a separate universe existed,
begotten through craftsmanship and creativity.
A water jug transformed into a pool with trout and willow.
A beaker contained a lichen-covered world of stone and
damp.
The Garden of Eden was enclosed in the silver gilt lining
of a rosewater dish.

I drank it all in 'til I was full to the brim and overflowing.
The silver creased my skin, seamed my veins and
enamelled my bones.
I was raised and chased, scored and folded, pierced and
burnished.

I left the cave a short time later and stood blinking in the
harsh daylight, hoping the curator wouldn't hear the
chink and clink of the treasure as I made my escape.
All that I left in that darkened space were metal
changelings whose forms will slowly fade and further
fade 'til they are just base memories.

TRANSPORTED

She stands square to the pavement
in sensible shoes,
a middle aged woman
with faded brown hair.
The Luas is late but she doesn't mind.
Adjusting her ballgown of taffeta blue,
she waits for the band to begin.

The Luas arrives and slides to a halt.
She gathers her bags up
and moves with the crowd
until she's inside.
The Luas is packed but she doesn't mind.
Along with the other finely dressed dancers,
she moves and sways with the music.

Seven stops later and close now to home,
she buttons her coat up
and checks for her keys.
The tiredness hits her.
The Luas stops and she steps through the door.
Hurrying for home before it gets dark,
she loses one small glass slipper.

ALL THE GOOD WORDS

All the good words have been used up already,
like 'blossom' and 'laden' and 'filter' and 'bough'.
Earlier today I sat under a tree and watched the sun
through the branches. I wanted to use the word 'canopy'
but no word could touch the pleasure I felt
being warmed by the sun in the shade of a tree.
No word could touch the brief symmetry
of the tree being there and the sun and the me.

DIMINISHED

"It's just a routine operation
and I'll be in and out in the one day."
But routine became serious
when 'drilling through bone' was mentioned.

He had to wait a week for the surgery
and sit around in pyjamas and slippers,
apologising to everyone for the inconvenience of it.
He charmed all of the nurses.

He was never one for drama
so we took our lead from him
and kept things light and low key.
It all felt quite unreal.

The surgery took forever.
He had to go under a second time.
We held our collective breath
and waited for him to break the surface.

That night the doctor rang.
"He's back in his bed asleep.
Come and see him in the morning.
He'll be ready for you then".

He was sitting out when we arrived,
awake, alert and doing the crossword.
He could have been at home,
except for the side of his head.

"You'll have to cancel the funeral,
sorry to disappoint you".
He was so much his usual self,
whole and undiminished.

But something was missing.
The childish certainty that
my parents would live forever.
The surgeon's knife had removed it.

MEMORIES

I remember my mother when she was a girl.
One day she was sad so I held her small hand.
I pulled her close but she faded away
and my arms hung empty by my side.

I met my father when he was seventeen.
He was running away from the red bricked house.
I tried to keep up but he ran too fast.
"Daddy," I shouted. He didn't look back.

I lay beside a dark-haired child.
She was watching shadows play games on the wall.
To keep her safe I sang a soft song.
Sleep came and carried her far away.

When I was old and close to death
A memory flashed across my mind.
A woman was moving through a music-filled room.
She caught my hand and pulled me close

And we danced and we danced and we danced.

CAN I TELL YOU ABOUT MY LOVES?

Can I tell you about my loves?
Each one, a new territory,
a virgin land rich in natural resources.
They are both present and future,
a timeline extending further than the eye can see.
They dream in vibrant colour.
My blood remembers them,
remembers crossing through membrane
to curl up inside each perfect life forming.
Their supple limbs are a constant wonder.
Stretching, striving, expanding,
they leave me breathless.
There is nothing on this sweet earth
to equal my love for them.
Life's longing for itself consummated
once, twice, three times, four times.
Can I tell you about my loves?

BETWEEN US

There was just fifteen months between us
and every early memory holds his imprint.
The smell of his skin I took as my own.

A snap shot.

We are four and five in a long back garden
that holds our whole universe.
We crouch, bony knees touching
and build our very first spider house.

There was only an inch between us
but that gave him the edge and the right
to be first at everything.

A memory

Mammy brings me up to his classroom
and I root around the desk for a souvenir
to bring home from this strange land.
The tide has brought him far from home
and I am waiting on the shore for a wave to pull me in.

There was only the landing between us
and when he was scared
we would whisper across the night-time divide.

A confession

Lying in the dark listening to his voice
that lacked its daytime authority,
I relished my power and stretched a full inch taller in the
bed.
I sometimes pretended to be asleep, just to hear his plea.

There was more than a foot between us
and from that distance
his words were muffled and hard to follow.

An observation

During adolescence I used his progress
as a yardstick for what success meant.
The bulk of his six-foot frame obscured my field of vision.
I chose only to see pint-sized dreams.

In early adulthood there was a continent between us,
and I stretched my unused wings
and discovered I could fly.

A one sided conversation

As I swooped and soared a voice inside me said
"Good but not good enough, bold but not bold enough"
It sounded just like his voice
and I did not question its credentials.

When he returned, our different lives lay between us
and we discovered that a shared beginning
does not ensure a lifelong bond.

A realisation

It's like I'm visiting a familiar country
but all the old places have been pulled down.
The map I've brought is obsolete
and I feel heavy with a peculiar sadness.

And now there is only a table between us
as we nurse our drinks and
keep an eye on the time.

A question

I wonder which one of us is on that far distant shore?
And if a tide can bring us back
to that time when we were 'the small ones',
a self-contained unit in a world of our own?

THE WORLD REDUCED TO SOUND

Lying in my single bed,
a childhood illness for company,
the world reduced to sound.

Behind my eyes the darkness echoed,
inside my chest uneven notes
rattled and wheezed.
Beyond my room a floorboard creaked,
a muffled cough across the landing
grew faint and faded away.

My hot ear pressed against the pillow
tuned into the gallop of tiny hooves,
then blessed, sleepy silence.
In the morning
steady, maternal footsteps
sang on the stairs.
I loved that song.

POST EXCAVATION ANALYSIS (AND A LITTLE GUESSWORK)

They were found in an old envelope,
two miniature handmade postcards,
perfectly sized and perfectly measured
to rest inside a small child's hand.

Cut precisely from thin cardboard,
One still bore the trace of a pencil line,
a faded testament to preparation,
carefully drawn to guide the scissors.

On the flip side there's a detailed picture,
Complete with hills and a dipping sun.
In the distance, a house with a smoking chimney,
the sky is shaded with purple and blue.

The second one shows a little girl,
with a white sailor's dress
and Shirley Temple curls.
I think she is standing in a park.

On the back there's a message,
just like a real postcard.
It's signed 'Your loving sister Joan',
an adult greeting in a childish script.

The other looks more rushed,
with an unexpected spelling mistake.
I'm guessing she wrote this one last,
her enthusiasm waning,

or maybe she was called for dinner
and polite and punctual as ever,
she finished up quickly and went inside,
wishing her hair would bounce as she walked.

BY THE TIME I GOT THERE

By the time I got there,
she'd been dead about two hours.
The nursing staff hovered their sympathy
as they ushered me in.
They left us alone together.
Her body still held the faint memory of warmth
and my fingers knew her skin
as they stroked her peaceful face.
Two aides came in to check on us.
There was nothing she needed now.
We could do no more for her.
Perhaps a last act of duty?

We could dress her for the journey.
Together we chose her garments,
 a peach blouse that she loved,
soft trousers, a cream cardigan.
With slow and gentle movements
we performed this final, intimate ritual,
murmuring endearments and soft apologies
when we couldn't get her arm into the sleeve.
She lay with her aged body like a new born babe
a dusting of talcum powder across her ribs,
pronounced now after weeks of not eating.
After we had finished I noticed her feet looked cold
and nearly wept to think she would feel exposed or chilly,
even in death. So we rooted out a pair of fluffy, warm
socks and eased them onto her feet.
She was ready now.

I thanked these women who had helped me
to tend to her as a daughter might,
these women, like sisters as we carefully and tenderly
dressed my spinster aunt.
The act of love in all its forms creates family.
They left me to say goodbye.
Her cheek was now cold and strange to the touch.
I was the only one in the room.

The next day I saw the body embalmed.
There was nothing left of the woman I loved.
Nothing. Closing my eyes I imagined her
lying in the warmth of my memory,
snug and comfortable.
That's where she is lying now.

THE MEDICINE BAG

My daughter has the measles.
Flushed and feverish,
her teenage body shivers and sweats
its way back to childhood.

Measles. Illness. Possible complications.
My mind runs round in circles
until memory reaches out
to guide my hand,

placing it on my daughter's brow
and from there the knowledge
comes flooding back,
only this time, it's me

carrying the medicine bag
of fresh, untangled sheets
and a wet, cold cloth
to cool her down.

Delving in further,
I find reassurances that say
the world still spins
and will wait for her.

This ritual laying on of hands,
these softly spoken incantations,
bind us both to a form of healing
passed on through textured tone and touch.

She is sleeping now,
the rash less red and frightening,
the rasping cough is muted,
her breathing deep and steady.

Lined up on her dresser
talismans stand guard,
flat 7up, paracetamol and cough bottle.
They protect her in my absence.

THE GREAT ESCAPE PART 1

He's very busy these days, beavering away just under the
radar.
Up in the attic with only a computer for company,
A devious plan is being hatched.
He's tunnelling his way out of a nine to five job.
Twenty nine years of soil and debris weigh heavy on his
shoulders but he's strong and built for digging.
The guards suspect nothing.

Last summer he made a run for freedom, almost reaching
the electric fence.
Through the wire he could see an open road like a
welcome invitation.
He could smell green grass and hear the birds singing in
the trees.
He listened to his heart beating wildly.

With the spotlight they found him, dragged him back to
his cell and cut his rations.
But what the guard failed to notice as he turned the key
and walked away was the sound of a small bird singing
inside the cell.
The singing tells our hero that freedom is just a shovelful
of earth away.
Humming under his breath he digs through the night and
in the morning hides the evidence of his labour.
In the exercise yard, he shakes his trousers and releases a
shower of earth right under their noses.

It is tiring, back breaking work but one fine day, when he least expects it, the tunnel will be finished.

He'll crawl through the tight space inch by inch.

The small bird, a beacon of sound, will guide him through darkness until fresh air and light welcome him.

A motorbike and the open road are standing side by side, waiting.

He'll put on his leather jacket, rev that engine 'til it purrs and take off without a backward glance.

LET IT BREATHE

Let it breathe a little, give it space.
Clear the path of stones and debris.
Release the tension that sits in your chest
and watch the fall and rise and fall again.
Everything in its own time and place.

Each action begins with an impulse
to move or change what is to what will be
and what will be is a dream-capped mountain.
I see a tiny figure resting at the summit,
arms reaching up to the airy, endless sky.

SHE'S BEEN HERE BEFORE

'Write a poem for me.' she commands her mother.
So I do.
Here it is.

From the moment she opened her birth coloured eyes
and drew us in, like moths to a flame,
we knew we were in trouble.

From the day she smiled knowingly
at just three weeks, wooing her public,
we knew our days were numbered.

At school she agreed an arrangement with the staff.
They could pretend to be in charge
and she would go along with them, for now.

At home she took on the might of two older sisters
and though they may win the occasional battle
(She'll show you her scars), the war is hers for the taking,

for she is the girl who has been here before
and knows the way like the back of her hand.
If we ask her nicely, maybe she'll draw us a map?

JOURNEY

In the last year my dad has really slowed up
so when I am out, I have taken to carrying him with me.
His dozing form on the couch hardly notices he's gone.

We stroll down familiar roads, over the Luas tracks
and past the red-bricked house he grew up in
on the corner of Bulfin road, then on down the hill,
up past the Royal hospital and turn left
into Memorial Gardens down at Islandbridge.

Once there he's a changed man
and we hurry past Trinity boat house,
following the small path that cuts through the grass
until we reach the water's edge. It's a hot summer's day
and there's a crowd of American visitors out on the river.
In one of the boats we spy a white-haired local boy.
One of the Americans throws him in and the boy learns to
swim on the way back to the bank.
Confident now he's in and out of the water like a pale sleek
seal and the sun and river reflect back the light coming
from him.
I somehow wish the boy were mine.

Then we wander up to the rose gardens
to unearth allotments buried just under the soil.
We sit basking on a bench, idly watching Mr Daly
from the South Circular Road, work his plot.
There's a neighbour's child with him,
helping to pull up vegetables and load them in a cart.
He is also loading up his mouth with
crunchy sweetheart cabbage
and thick stalks of raspberry red rhubarb.
When the thirst hits, he trots down to the railway track
beside the bridge where a spring gushes out of the wall
and into his cupped hands.
He returns to his work quenched and cooled.
The sun slips slowly down and Mr Daly
and the neighbour's boy start for home.
I would like to go some of the way with them.

Back on the couch Dad stirs and it's time for us to leave.
Rousing ourselves, we slowly wind our way along the edge
of the river bend, where memories lie curled,
soothed to sleep by the sound of oars slicing water.
Up ahead the road forks but for now
we walk along together towards the lessening light.

THE GREAT ESCAPE PART 2

It's easy for one person to escape.
A wire cutter and some tunnel vision should do the trick.
Any Tom, Dick or Harry could do it,
just find a blind spot and go for it.

It's getting everyone out that's difficult.
Risking the lives of others requires nerves of steel.
How can he tunnel under his responsibilities
without the walls caving in on top of them all?

That is the question that weighs him down
and fills his throat with sand and soil.
He imagines them caught in a web of barbed wire,
handcuffed to the life he's sentenced them to.

That question frog marches him into the cooler,
closes the door and turns the key.
Twenty days in isolation. Maybe he'll hit on the answer
with a glove and a ball?

HUGS

My son hugs me in the hall by the stairs,
an eleven year old tight hug.
He stands on the first step,
a thirteen year old quick hug.
He bounds up two steps,
a 'Rushing off, must go,' hug.
And on the fourth step,
a 'What's the weather like down there?' hug.

ALL GROWN UP

I can pinpoint the very moment
when adulthood greeted me.
I was well into my twenties and
had a small child or two in tow.
I wore the mantle of mother
but underneath I felt like a child.
It was all dress up and let's pretend
and hope that no one notices.
While down in the local shopping centre
with my dollies and buggy, playing 'Shop'
with monopoly money, I went into the butchers
for some play food and it happened.

There
amidst
the
sawdust
and
the
metallic
smell
of
blood

the butcher Fran said
"What can I get you today, Mrs Tannam?"
and I looked over my shoulder
to see if my Mam was there.
I was alone.

I turned back around to face him
and he was looking straight at me.
So I drew myself up and said with quiet authority,
"I'll have that piece of round steak there.
No, not that piece, the one to the left of it, please".
Then I paid him with my hard-earned cash,
zipped the children up against the cold
and headed back to my bricks and mortar house
where the rest of my life was waiting for me.

A HAIR'S BREATH

We walk side by side, chatting together about this team or
that player.
His warm hand slips into mine as we approach the
crossing,
a big hand that at ten, he has yet to grow into.
Then I hear and see the ambulance
turning abruptly left into Our Lady's hospital.
Some mother's son may never grow into
his beautiful strong hands.
I can almost touch that woman and feel the fear
tighten in her throat.
The wail of the siren fades and is swallowed up by the
passing traffic.
My shoulders relax and I remember to exhale
and then we are across the road and now we talk of
school.

LIKE THE SUN

The words, like the sun in a June Irish sky,
behind shape-changing clouds that pass by.
One cannot predict when the clouds will break up
and let the warmth seep through the skin,
allowing the language to bathe us in light,
and filter the meaning within.

SOME MORNINGS I WAKE

Some mornings I wake
and anxiety is lodged
in an unknown place
that I cannot access.

It carries within it
a sense of uncertainty,
a sense of not knowing
who I am meant to be.

It feels like a small child
is clinging too tightly.
My shoulders and arms ache
but I can't put her down.

I lie there a while.
I am filled with the feeling.
The clock speaks of duty
and hours and hours.

The longer I stay there
the heavier the child gets.
Some action is needed.
I throw back the duvet.

I get up.

And slowly work through
the layers of the morning,

and the rhythm of living
with its familiar refrain

persuades the small child
to loosen her grip.
I sense her absence
and my body grows lighter

with each task completed.
The clock speaks of lunchtime,
and the sound of its ticking
puts the small child to sleep.

I move carefully in case she wakes.

WAITING

He waits anxiously, hovering in my peripheral vision
for a sign, a signal. He is waiting for me to return.
He treads carefully, keeping the conversation neutral.
It is very hard work, filling in the awkward silences.
He cannot reach me.
I cannot help him.
For I do not know where I am or when I will return.
I wish that someday he would come and look for me,
that someday he would come and find me. I guess
we are both waiting.

THE GREAT ESCAPE PART 3

At first he dreamed of an easy escape.
He would slip away in the still of the night,
unnoticed, untouched, undamaged.

Now he looks at his hands,
calloused, bruised, bloodied,
but strong.
Grabbing the shovel, he heads back to the tunnel.
There's no time to lose when there's work to be done.

A LOPSIDED CONVERSATION

Me

How do I shut my eyes so I can see?
Stop up my ears so I can hear?
Close my mouth so I can speak?

How do I move between cloud and stone?
Learn to breathe on land and in water?
Measure the distance from here to there?

How do I sift through the hours and the days?
Sway to the rhythm of the influential moon?
Follow the will-o'-the-wisp in the dark?

How do I know when too much is too much?
When too little is too little?
When enough is enough?

The Universe

"ENOUGH. I can't get a word in edgeways"

TUNING IN

Woke up this morning and knew that today I could tune
into Station Universe.
I could tell by the quality of the 8am sunshine.
Dropping the tadpoles off at Ringsend pool for their
morning swim,
the pooch and I headed down to Sandymount,
hoping to tune into Station Universe on our travels
(She being of the low-slung variety, can pick up signals
running along the ground beneath our feet).

At first there was just the two of us and the sounds of the
day beginning,
my jacket rustling and Boo's small paws tap-tapping on
the tarmac,
light traffic in the distance and a soft breeze
teasing the dry, winter leaves.
We settled into our usual rhythm and the landscape
unfolded before our eyes and under our feet.

And then I felt a tilt, a shift so subtle perhaps I imagined
it?
All looked the same but in that sameness it had changed.
The morning became this morning, the first and last and
only morning.
Station Universe was transmitting on every frequency, on
every wavelength.
And it was EVERYWHERE and it was
EVERYTHING.

Walking through Irishtown Nature Reserve,
a robin redbreast winked at me and a sedate gaggle of
Brent Geese snacking beside the Pigeon House,
whispered cold Canadian tales to me.
Underfoot the sands crunched and crumbled
and I felt the earth shift on its axis.
Shells and seaweed washed up the beach
inted at life forms in a galaxy, deep, deep below,
but the whiff from the sewage plant brought me right
back to earth.

Leaving the strand behind us, we climbed onto the solid
granite of the South Wall.
For a while I lost the signal but followed the echo of
footsteps to Poolbeg Lighthouse.
Halfway down the wall, Dublin Bay threw her arms
round me.

and deep in the embrace, I heard a song of home.
The waters glimmered all round me
and November sunlight washed over me.

At Half-Moon Clubhouse we stopped and the past came
back to visit.
I saw four children in the late summer sun
and they were two years younger and noisier.
Boo was there too and my father's dog Sally and we three
basked in the sun
while the children splashed and shrieked and shouted their
truth.

Time moving on pulls me back and the rest of the day beckons.
Station Universe stops transmitting and the "what's for dinner?"
and the " Oh, it's late I better hurry" are all I can think about.

But here on the couch, my fingers moving on the keyboard,
I remember every little detail, though the words aren't enough to capture them all.
It's like scooping up a handful of seawater and now all that's left is the taste of salt on my fingers.

THE ART OF LISTENING

I'm not talking about a half-hearted,
catching the words but not the meaning
type of listening, that uses one ear
and the occasional "Oh, I see".
That type of listening you come across
everyday of the week

No, what I'm singing my hymn of praise to
is a higher form of communication altogether.
I'm talking about employing all the tools at our disposal,
two ears, two eyes, the heart, the gut,
that place inside where compassion and empathy lie.

I'm talking about a whole body receptor
tuning into what the speaker is saying,
not just to their voice but to the silence
when they pause to search for a word,
their eyes and body speaking
eloquently on their behalf.

Someone takes the risk of releasing the truth
of who they are into the care of another
and miracle of miracles, the other reaches out with both
hands,
cradles that truth, blesses it with acceptance,
enfolds it in acknowledgement, and tenderly gives it back
into the care of the one who gave it life.

Now, that type of listening is rare.
It's an art form, a sculptured moment of connection
inviting us to come inside and be astonished
at what the heart can hold.

THE START OF THE AFFAIR

She arrived on the last day of Spring,
a quantum leap of blind faith,
weighing just six pounds two ounces.
She stretched into her chosen name
and miraculously, the word became flesh.
Look, curled up inside a protective embrace,
the tiny girl is sleeping after her journey.
Her dazed parents gaze and gaze upon her.

HER ABSENCE

Her absence fills the room,
seeps under the door
and down a corridor
where nurses pass
with silent shoes
and heads bent low.

Inside the room
two parents sit,
her absence
wedged between them.
They speak in hushed
and stilted tones
to stop their grief from waking.

Her absence sleeps on and on,
oblivious to their presence.
How can something
so small and so perfect
be not tucked up
in the warm, woollen blanket?

I STAND OUTSIDE

Most days there lies a chasm between my thoughts
and the words that might bless them with meaning.
The harder I try to stretch across the divide,
the deeper and bigger the gap becomes.
But sometimes the words rush towards me
and gathering them up, I lay them out
like crazy paving stones, zigzagging down to a summer house
near the end of a garden.
I have no idea what is stored there
or what the view looks like from inside,
but enfolded in the musty fragrance of timber and trapped sunlight
is a voice so ordinary and yet so fragile
it could disintegrate.
I stand outside with cheek and ear pressed
against the warm wooden door and

                                        listen.

DOING HER THING

There she is,
doing her thing.
Here I am, just
watching her
doing her thing
with such graceful ease.

There she is,
doing her thing.
Here I am, just
admiring her
doing her thing
with such easeful grace.

There she is,
full to the brim.
Here I am, just
loving her.

CONSOLATION

In a claustrophobic room
just off intensive care,
he outlined the facts.

"She only scored four
on the Glasgow scale.
It's not looking good".

Even as he said it
I knew this moment
defined 'before' and 'after.'

I hyperventilated.
My mind looked on
as my body drowned.

We sat by her bed.
The word 'coma'
came and sat beside us.

That evening she awoke.
Everything had changed.
She saw her daddy cry.

But a lifelong disease
is so much better
than no life at all.

When we got home
The house had moved
To another galaxy.

Reclaimed

I want to reclaim some land that once belonged to me.
It was foolishly lost in the mad rush to be somewhere else.
Look, here is a rough map of the forgotten territory.
I keep it folded in my back pocket.

Peer into the patch of thick-branched bushes just behind
my parent's house.
There's a space inside that's filled with scratches and warm
silence.

In the corner of a garden is an apple tree with a bockity
swing.
The ground moves back and forth and back again. The
sky feels dizzy.

Follow the wall down to the boathouse that smells of tar
and seaweed.
The stones on the strand hold the warmth of endless
summer.

Far away from the familiar, in a kitchen on the North
coast,
is the smell of soda bread and the first wild taste of
freedom.

Across the cola-coloured stream that is hidden in a crease
runs a path through lilac heather, soft and springy to the
touch.

I was once queen of this odd-shaped corner Kingdom
but I chose to live in exile in a land that's not my own.
Some day when I muster up the strength,
I'll march straight back in and reclaim my empty throne.

CHRISTMAS EVE

And now at last, it's Christmas Eve.
The carousel of endless preparation stops and we get off,
dizzy from all that forward motion. Time slows down and
catching breath
we look and see that everything is as it should be,
the smells, the lights, the Christmas tree and underneath,
with a red bow tied, the gift of anticipation.

Children wrapped in new pyjamas with glittering eyes and
tinselled toes
begin the countdown dance of 'One More Sleep' and
catching our hands
they pull us along through those silly, precious, time-
honoured rituals
that recreate the holy blessed sacrament of Christmas Eve,
until bedtime comes
and, one by one, stockings are hung and reluctant children
are sent off to begin the arduous task of trying to sleep so
that morning can come.

And then there's just the two of us, Santa and his missus
with one or two
little jobs to do before we can call it a day. From their
hiding places
presents appear and arrange themselves into four, fat piles
and mysterious,
odd-shaped, small-sized gifts slide into stockings and jostle
for space before settling down.
The room is ready and look, the clock hands bring us

tidings of great joy,
it is tomorrow and Santa has come. One last quick check
that everything is in its place,
then lights off, cat out, lock the door, climb the stairs and
after a long, long day
spent miles apart, head and pillow reunite.

And in a manger far away a baby boy is born.

THE WOMAN IN THE MIRROR

Ten years ago I bought a dress in T.K.Maxx.
It was like nothing I had owned before.
I remember trying it on just for fun
and staring at the woman in the mirror.
She dared me to go ahead and buy it.

It lived in the wardrobe for a year,
waiting for the chance to show off.
We just needed the right occasion.
The see-through plastic covering crinkled
each time I reached for my jeans.

A friend rang and asked to borrow it.
She had an occasion but no dress.
When she came over to try it on,
the three of us agreed it was a perfect fit.
I stood at the door and waved them off.

Then back it went into the wardrobe.
Until many years later,
I decided to have it taken up
so I could wear it to a Christmas party.
Finally, we could all go out together.

Wriggling into the altered dress,
I stood in front of the mirror.
The woman looked me right in the eye
and told me what I already knew.
The romance was long over.

The dress still hangs in the wardrobe,
a measuring tape for my daughters.
Each year they blossom more
and the woman in the mirror
dares them to strut their stuff.

CURRICULUM VITAE

I was born just down the road from here, south of my
mother.
A shape-changer by trade, a chameleon by choice.
Sometimes I do a bit of this, sometimes I do a bit of that,
sometimes I do a bit of doing nothing at all.
I have ups and downs and roundabouts
and backwards and forwards and standing still.
The body I inhabit is a sound one, a comfortable one,
with adjustable arms for embracing.
I believe in believing.
And stopping every once in a while.
When I grow up I want to be.

I am.

In an Ocean of Ignorance

I swim in a sea of ignorance.
What I don't know, if it were an iceberg,
would sink the Titanic
and I still couldn't tell you
what tune they were playing when
"Oops", she went over and under.

I stroll through the meadow of oblivion
where the sum of my forgetfulness
is greater than all the blades of grass growing.
Ahh there's a lovely yellow whatchmacallit,
close to that thingamajig just over there.

I float in a galaxy of 'It's just on the tip of my tongue and
at three o'clock in the morning it'll come to me'
and I couldn't say, with any degree of certainty,
what planet is closest to the sun.

But I know what I know.
I know this life is blessed.
I remember to give praise.